THE 40 DAYS Experience

PRAYER & FASTING JOURNAL

• • ● • •

The Fulfillment of Promise

Crossroads Christian Church, Corona, CA
Visit us for live services at www.CrossroadsChurch.com

ISBN-13:
978-1522923770

ISBN-10:
1522923772

Dedication

I want to dedicate this journal to our Crossroads Christian Church family. I love their passion for Christ, His Cause and His Community. I love they consistently desire to go deeper in their relationship with God.

I want to thank Taleah Murray, Kasey Husen, and EJ Romero for working so hard to bring this journal from a dream to a reality.

Contents

• • ● • •

The Fulfillment of Promise

I am excited that you are ready to embark on a 40-day journey with God! 40 is a significant number that God uses throughout the Bible as a sign of the fulfillment of His promises.

- Moses fasted for 40 days while on the mountain with God before he received the 10 commandments and the design of the tabernacle.
- Jesus fasted for 40 days before He began His ministry.
- Jesus was on the earth 40 days after he rose from the dead before he ascended to Heaven to be with God.

As you embark on this 40 day journey with God, ask Him to enact His promises in your life.

Fasting intensifies our prayer life because it causes us to pray with intentionality. When we crave what we have chosen to fast from, it reminds us to seek the Lord in prayer. The more we crave what satisfies our flesh, the more we seek God to satisfy our souls. My prayer for you is that over these next 40 days, you have a life-changing encounter with your Heavenly Father.

During these next 40 days I want to encourage you to fast from something, for something, and for someone.

Fast From Something:

The best way to know what to fast from is to ask God for guidance. Ask God specifically what He wants you to give up. It should be something that you will miss daily, however be mindful that the goal of the fast is not to torture yourself, but rather to focus on God.

A good Biblical example of someone who practiced fasting correctly is Daniel. In the book of Daniel, Daniel chose to deny himself a fleshly desire for a defined period of time. Daniel and his friends fasted from "choice food" and wine and ate only vegetables for 10 days. In Daniel 10 we see that he chose to fast from tasty food, wine, and bathing for 21 days (I wouldn't recommend fasting from deodorant or bathing!)

Pray for God to guide you to what He wants you to fast from.

Fast For Something:

I am going to sound like a broken record here, but again, the best way to know what to fast for is to ask God. Psalm 37:4 says, *"Delight yourself in the Lord and He will give you the desires of your heart."* God is a loving Father who wants to bless His children. Hebrews 11:6 states that God is a rewarder of those who seek Him. The book of James describes how God blesses us with good and perfect gifts. One of the reasons we do not receive what God desires to give us is because we do not ask.

Here are some suggestions of things you could fast for during this 40 day fast:

- A heart's desire
- God's clear direction on a decision you need to make
- A breakthrough you need in your life
- Freedom from bondage (addiction, anxiety, anger etc.)

Fast For Someone:

All Christians are commissioned to go into the world and make disciples. Jesus expects us to share in His cause, which is to seek and save the lost. It is our job to go and tell others about Him so that they can experience His love and the life transformation that He brings. Who are you telling about Jesus? Who do you want to see come to know the Lord for the first time or return to Him? During these next 40 days we need to intentionally and passionately pray for these specific people whom Jesus loves so much to come to know Him!

Write down...

- What you are fasting from?

- What you are fasting for?

- Who are you fasting for?

Six Aspects of Biblical Fasting

There are six aspects of Biblical fasting: Discipline, Focus, Celebration, Purpose, Generosity, & Promise.

1) Discipline of Fasting

> *"Why have we fasted and You do not see? Why have we humbled ourselves and You do not notice? 'Behold, on the day of your fast you find your desire, And drive hard all your workers.*
>
> *Behold, you fast for contention and strife and to strike with a wicked fist. You do not fast like you do today to make your voice heard on high." Isaiah 58:3-4*

The people of Israel were asking God why He had not heard their prayers when they fasted. God's response is that He heard their requests but that their behavior in the midst of the fast was not acceptable to Him. They used the fast as an excuse to be irritable and mean spirited.

Ramadan is the ninth month of the Islamic calendar and is marked by a month long fast where the Muslim people fast daily from food and drink from sun up to sun down and at night they feast. An Islamic friend of mine who lives in Israel informed me that Ramadan is his least favorite time of the year because the Muslim people are irritable, unfriendly, and angry during that month and the whole town is negatively affected!

We can be the same way when we fast if we are not careful. During a fast, you are to abstain from doing or eating something that is a part of your daily life. It should be something that hurts to give up because that pain will remind you to pray and connect with God on a daily basis.

I will be fasting from sweets and carbohydrates during this fast and as you can imagine, that has the potential to make a person quite irritable! My sinful nature manifests itself as impatience, crankiness, and edginess. When I sense my sinful nature, rearing its ugly head, I must be disciplined to choose the fruit of the Spirit rather than the fruit of the flesh. When we fast, we must train ourselves to act in righteousness and Christ-likeness.

"Then Jesus said to His disciples, 'If anyone wishes to come after Me, he must deny himself, and take up his cross and follow Me.'"
Matthew 16:24

Fasting is beneficial because we practice denying self and following Christ.

2) Focus of Fasting

While fasting, God wants us to abide with Him. Practically speaking, "abiding with Him" looks like focused, intentional, and continual prayer. In doing this, we become more like Him and His love is perfected in us.

> *"We have come to know and have believed the love which God has for us. God is love, and the one who abides in love abides in God, and God abides in him.*
>
> *By this, love is perfected with us, so that we may have confidence in the day of judgment; because as He is, so also are we in this world."*
> *1 John 4:16-17*

Jesus says that when we abide in Him, we will bear fruit and live a life of significance.

> *"Abide in Me, and I in you. As the branch cannot bear fruit of itself unless it abides in the vine, so neither can you unless you abide in Me.*
>
> *I am the vine, you are the branches; he who abides in Me and I in him, he bears much fruit, for apart from Me you can do nothing."*
> *John 15:4-5*

Fasting shifts our focus from wordly things to God Himself. In doing this, we become more aware of His presence, we learn to abide in Him, and we live fruitful lives.

3) Celebration of Fasting

In the book of Isaiah, the prophet Isaiah points out to the people that God is not answering their prayers because they are fasting as a means of mourning rather than fasting as a means of celebrating.

> *"Is it a fast like this which I choose, a day for a man to humble himself? Is it for bowing one's head like a reed and for spreading out sackcloth and ashes as a bed? Will you call this a fast, even an acceptable day to the LORD? Isaiah 58:5*

When we fast we celebrate that we get to spend more intentional time with God and grow closer to Him. We should not walk around hanging our heads low, sulking and miserable. In the book of Matthew, Jesus tells us to snap out of our self-pity and celebrate instead.

> *"Whenever you fast, do not put on a gloomy face as the hypocrites do, for they neglect their appearance so that they will be noticed by men when they are fasting. Truly I say to you, they have their reward in full.*

> *"But you, when you fast, anoint your head and wash your face so that your fasting will not be noticed by men, but by your Father who is in secret; and your Father who sees what is done in secret will reward you. Matthew 6:16-18*

During a fast we are to have a good attitude and celebrate, because being in the presence of God and abiding with Him is worthy of celebration.

4) The Purpose of the Fasting

Isaiah tells us that fasting brings freedom from the bondage of sin. We are to see freedom from habits that are not holy or healthy.

> *"Is this not the fast which I choose, To loosen the bonds of wickedness, To undo the bands of the yoke, And to let the oppressed go free And break every yoke?" Isaiah 58:6*

Fasting strengthens self-control, which is one of the fruits of the Spirit. By practicing self-control, we overcome fleshly desires and instead pursue Godly desires. We find ourselves more aligned with Him and begin to pray for others to experience this same freedom from bondage and alignment with God.

5) Generosity of Fasting

> *"Is it not to divide your bread with the hungry And bring the homeless poor into the house; When you see the naked, to cover him; And not to hide yourself from your own flesh?" Isaiah 58:7*

In this Scripture, Isaiah is telling the people of Israel to provide for those in need during their fast. As we fast and tune in to the heart of Christ, He opens our eyes to the physical needs of people and He wants us to meet those needs.

This is a tough concept for me to personally grasp because I am naturally a selfish person. I find myself fighting against generosity. For example, if there is someone begging for money at a freeway off ramp, I have a tendency to ignore them. However, I know that God is a generous God and that I need to be generous as well. During this particular time of fasting, my wife and I will be saving money because we will be eating out less! We have decided to set that saved money aside to give to people in need. Each day that I fast I ask God to show me who I can bless that day and I ask Him to help me be generous. In doing this, I find myself overflowing with joy.

6) Promise of Fasting

When we fast correctly, God promises us answered prayers, invigoration, joy, guidance, strength, protection, and fulfillment.

> "Then your light will break out like the dawn, And your recovery will speedily spring forth; And your righteousness will go before you; The glory of the LORD will be your rear guard.
>
> Then you will call, and the LORD will answer; You will cry, and He will say, 'Here I am.' If you remove the yoke from your midst, The pointing of the finger and speaking wickedness,
>
> And if you give yourself to the hungry And satisfy the desire of the afflicted, Then your light will rise in darkness And your gloom will become like midday.
>
> And the LORD will continually guide you, And satisfy your desire in scorched places, And give strength to your bones; And you will be like a watered garden, And like a spring of water whose waters do not fail.
>
> Those from among you will rebuild the ancient ruins; You will raise up the age-old foundations; And you will be called the repairer of the breach, The restorer of the streets in which to dwell." Isaiah 58:8-12

Discipline
Focus · Celebration
Purpose · Generosity
Promise

Using this Journal

Step 1: Set an Appointment

Just as you would schedule a meeting into your calendar, you need to schedule a set time to meet with the Lord. This is part of being "intentional." If you do not plan for this time, it will never be a priority. Planning sets you up for success.

> *"The plans of the diligent lead surely to abundance, but everyone who is hasty comes only to poverty." Proverbs 21:5 (ESV)*

Set a time to meet with the Lord daily and follow through. I prefer to spend the first part of my day with Him, but that does not work for Everyone. Find the time of day that works for you, and commit to spending that portion of your day with God.

Step 2: Pray

Start each session with a conversation with your Father in Heaven. There is no need to use pretentious language to try to impress God. Intimate relationships are relationships where you can be yourself, so be yourself when spending this time with Him. I like to take a walk and talk to God about the weather, or why my plants are not growing, or about my grandchildren. I talk to Him about my hopes and dreams. I talk to Him about what I am facing that day. At the end of this prayer time, free yourself from distractions and ask God to open your eyes to what He wants to teach you that day.

> *"But the anointing that you received from him abides in you, and you have no need that anyone should teach you. But as his anointing teaches you about everything, and is true, and is no lie—just as it has taught you, abide in him." 1 John 2:27 (ESV)*

God promises to use the Holy Spirit to teach you. Although, we are to have human teachers, we answer ultimately only to God. While it is good to hear solid Biblical teaching, we need to seek God and His Spirit to show us what is true. As you study, trust that He will guide and teach you.

Step 3: Read the Passage and Answer the Questions

The questions are designed to help you get a better understanding of what God is saying in the Scriptures. Some passages have imagery that applies to our lives today. Be sure to write down what the imagery means in that setting and time and then how it applies to your life. Look for things that the passages say God wants us to do and the things He wants us to avoid. Most of all, pay attention to the promises God makes to His people that apply to us today

Step 4: Write Out a Prayer to God

Writing out your prayers to God is a great way to pray. The book of Psalms is essentially David's written prayers to God. This is a great way to remember what you have prayed for and to see how God answers those prayers. As you watch Him answer your requests, your faith will grow, and you will be filled with joy. One of my favorite promises that God makes in His Word is found in Jeremiah 33. says,

"Call to Me and I will answer you, and I will tell you great and mighty things, which you do not know." Jeremiah 33:3

Many times throughout my life I have called out to God, and many times He has followed through and shown me "great and mighty things" which I had not known prior to calling out to Him. I hope that during this 40 Day journey you will boldly call out to God, and that He will show you great and mighty things!

Day 1 Read Psalm 1

What does the Blessed man not do?

_____

_____

_____

_____

What does the Blessed man do?

_____

_____

_____

_____

Write out each of the promises found in verse 3 and what they mean.

_____

_____

_____

_____

_____

Ask God if you are making decisions based on the counsel or advice you have received from ungodly people.

_____

_____

_____

_____

Ask God if there are people in your life that you should not be around.

_____

_____

_____

_____

Ask God if you are being judgmental toward others or having a negative attitude that is limiting your faith in Him and what He will do.

....

....

....

....

....

Write out a prayer for what you are fasting for and who you are fasting for.

....

....

....

....

....

Day 2 Read Jeremiah 17:1-18

According to verses 5-6 what brings a curse on us?

....

....

....

....

....

....

Write out each part of the curse found in verse 6 and what God is saying this curse will look like and feel like in your life.

....

....

....

....

....

....

According to verses 7-8 what causes us to be blessed?

....

....

....

....

....

....

Write out each of the promises found in verse 8 and what the promise will look like and feel like in your life.

....

....

....

....

....

What do verses 9-10 tell you about your heart (your feelings and emotions)?

....

....

....

....

....

As you read 11-18 what stands out to you?

....

....

....

....

In light of what you have read, are you someone who relies too much on people, makes decisions based on emotions or is too tied to money?

....

....

....

....

....

Pray and ask God if anything mentioned in the previous question has a hold on your life. Then write down what you sense God is telling you.

....

....

....

....

Day 3 Read Psalm 37

Write down what God does not want you to do.

_____

_____

_____

_____

_____

Write down what God wants you to do and the promised results.

_____

_____

_____

_____

_____

_____

Of the things that God does not want you to do, are there some that are particularly difficult for you to control?

_____

_____

_____

_____

_____

Summarize what this Psalm tells you about the righteous.

_____

_____

_____

_____

_____

_____

Summarize what this Psalm tells you about the wicked.

....

....

....

....

....

Are there some situations, relationships or areas of your life that you need to commit to the Lord?

....

....

....

....

....

Day 4   Read Psalm 51

The context of this Psalm is that it was written after Nathan exposed David's adultery and he was publicly humiliated.

What does David say about sin?

What does David ask God to do for him?

What does David say he will do in response to God answering his prayers?

In light of this, ask God if there is any sin in you that you need to confess to Him and to others. Write down what He brings to mind.

_____

_____

_____

_____

_____

_____

Day 5   Read Psalm 91

How does knowing that this Psalm is talking about Spiritual Warfare enlighten your understanding of the passage?

_____

_____

_____

_____

_____

Write down what God protects you from and how He protects you?

_____

_____

_____

_____

_____

In verses 14-16 God is talking to us. What does God promise to do for those who love and trust Him?

_____

_____

_____

_____

_____

Looking at verse 14, why does God deliver us from the enemy and put us securely on high?

_____

_____

_____

_____

_____

Write down the things you tend to be afraid of or worry about.

....

....

....

....

....

....

....

Now, write out a prayer asking God to protect you and provide for you in each of those areas. Be specific in what you are asking Him to do.

....

....

....

....

....

....

Day 6 Read Deuteronomy 10:12-22

This was what God wanted the people to know before they entered the Promised Land. These same principles apply to you as you enter into the promises that God has for you. In verses 10-13 God tells you what He expects from you. Write those expectations down.

_____

_____

_____

_____

_____

What do you think is the significance of the order that God puts these expectations in?

_____

_____

_____

_____

_____

_____

Why does God want you to do these expectations?

_____

_____

_____

_____

_____

In verses 14-22 write down each thing the Lord is calling for us to be or to do.

_____

_____

_____

_____

_____

Ask God to make you aware if you are not being faithful in any of the attitudes or actions He is calling for you to do.

_____

_____

_____

_____

_____

_____

Day 7 Read John 14

What does Jesus tell us about Himself?

What does Jesus say we will do if we love Him?

In Verse 21 write down the three specific promises Jesus makes to us.

What does this chapter tell you about the Holy Spirit?

Pray, asking Jesus to disclose Himself during the rest of this fast.

_____

_____

_____

_____

_____

_____

_____

Day 8   Read 1 Corinthians 2:6-16

We are told in verse 9 that God wants to give things to you and do things for you that are beyond our ability to see, describe or imagine. Who will He do this for?

According to verses 10-13, how does God reveal these things to us?

What do verses 14-16 tell you regarding how the Holy Spirit reveals what God wants to give you and what God wants to do for you?

Have you already experienced God giving you things that are beyond description and beyond imagination? If so write down what God did and what happened when He did it.

Pray and ask God to use the Holy Spirit to reveal to you the wonderful things He has for you during this fast.

_____

_____

_____

_____

_____

_____

Day 9 Read 1 Kings 19

To help you further understand 1 Kings 19: 12, you need to know the different bible translations. The New American Standard Version has the translation, "a gentle blowing." The New Living Translation reads, "the sound of a gentle whisper." The English Standard Version states, "sound of a low whisper." The New King James Version reads, "a still small voice."

....

....

....

....

....

How did God speak to Elijah in verses 12-13?

....

....

....

....

....

In verse 10 we see Elijah felt depressed and alone. Now that God has his attention what does he learn in verse 18?

....

....

....

....

....

Knowing Elijah felt alone and in despair, what does the last line of this chapter tell you regarding how God gave Elijah something beyond description and beyond imagination?

....

....

....

....

....

In light of what you have learned the last three days, pray and ask God to make you sensitive to the gentle whisper of the Holy Spirit during this fast.

_____

_____

_____

_____

_____

Day 10 Read John 3:1-21

What does Jesus tell us about being Born Again

....

....

....

....

....

What does Jesus tell us about God's love and God's judgment?

....

....

....

....

....

....

What does verse 8 tell you about the Holy Spirit?

....

....

....

....

....

Look back over your notes from Day 8 and 9. How do these fit with what you see in verse 8?

....

....

....

....

....

....

Pray and ask God to reveal to you the times you could not see Him; yet as the invisible blowing of the wind can be felt and it's effects can be seen, God was there with you. Write down any moments that come to mind.

_____

_____

_____

_____

_____

Pray and ask God to make you sensitive to Him and the moving of the Holy Spirit during this fast.

_____

_____

_____

_____

_____

Day 11 Read Job 33

What does verse 14 tell you about our relationship with God?

_____

_____

_____

_____

_____

Read verses 15-23 and write down some of the ways God speaks to us.

_____

_____

_____

_____

_____

_____

_____

Read verses 24-26 and write down what we pray as we intercede for another person.

_____

_____

_____

_____

_____

Pray and ask God to make you aware of when and how He is speaking to you.

_____

_____

_____

_____

_____

Pray a prayer of intercession for the person you are fasting for.

_____

_____

_____

_____

_____

Day 12 Read Isaiah 40

What does verse 8 tell you about God's Word?

_____

_____

_____

_____

_____

What do verses 10-17 reveal to you about God?

_____

_____

_____

_____

_____

What do verses 28-29 tell you about God?

_____

_____

_____

_____

_____

_____

What does God promise to those who trust in God or wait on Him?

_____

_____

_____

_____

_____

In light of what God promises in verses 29-31, pray asking God to make each of the promises true in your life during this fast.

_____

_____

_____

_____

_____

_____

Day 13 Read Proverbs 3:1-10

What do verses 1-4 tell you to do and what will be the result?

What do verses 5-10 tell you to do and what will be the results?

Look back at verses 5 and 6 and ask God to unveil to you if there is any area of your life that you are not trusting in Him completely.

Look at what you learned in verses 9-10. "Honor the Lord from your wealth" means to give an offering to God. Pray and ask God to reveal to you what amount you should give as an offering to Him at the end of the fast.

From "the first of all your produce" means to give a tithe of the first 10% of any income you receive. Pray and tell God you trust Him completely and will commit to being faithful to tithe to Him the first %10 of the income you receive.

Day 14 Read Psalm 25

What does David ask God to do in verses 1-7?

What are we told God will do for us in verses 8-13?

Now read this Psalm praying it as a personal prayer for you. Write down what comes to mind as you pray it.

Write out a very specific prayer asking God to provide what you are fasting for.

Write out a prayer asking God to move in the life for the person you are fasting for.

....

....

....

....

....

....

Day 15 Read James 1

What are we told to do during times of trial and testing in James 1:2-5 and verses 12-13?

What does God promise to do if we ask Him in verses 5-7?

How is faith and prayer linked in verses 5-7?

In verses 19-20 what are we told we are to know and do?

In verses 21-25 what are we told regarding how we are to apply God's Word to our lives?

In verses 26-27 what are we told the religion God loves is like?

_____

_____

_____

_____

_____

After reading this practical and powerful chapter, pray and ask God to reveal to you anything you need to stop doing or start doing that will cause you to be a "doer" of the Word and not only a "hearer."

_____

_____

_____

_____

_____

Day 16 Read Mark 11

Focus on verses 22-26.

_____

_____

_____

_____

_____

_____

What does Jesus tell us to do when we pray?

_____

_____

_____

_____

_____

What does Jesus promise you if you pray this way?

_____

_____

_____

_____

_____

Write out a prayer believing that God will answer you regarding the "something" you
are fasting for. Write down what you believe it will be like when He does.

_____

_____

_____

_____

Ask God to bring to mind anyone you need to forgive and commit to truly forgive them.

_____

_____

_____

_____

_____

Pray for the person you are fasting for. Write down what it will be like when God answers that prayer.

_____

_____

_____

_____

_____

Day 17 Read Luke 18:1-30

Write down what verses 1-17 tell you about how we should pray.

_____

_____

_____

_____

_____

_____

What does verse 27 tell you about God?

_____

_____

_____

_____

_____

_____

What do verses 28-30 tell you God will do for you if you are completely committed to Him?

_____

_____

_____

_____

_____

Write down some of the ways God has already blessed you.

_____

_____

_____

_____

_____

_____

Write out a prayer asking God to reveal to you all the things He has for you during this fast. Ask Him for the "something" you are fasting for; ask Him for the "someone" you are fasting for.

_____

_____

_____

_____

_____

_____

Day 18 Read Luke 11:1-13

According to verses 1-4, what should you ask for and how should you ask?

In verses 5-8 what is needed with the way we pray?

What does Jesus promise in verses 9-10?

In verse 9-10, what are the three action words Jesus tells us to do regarding how we pray?

What do verses 11-13 tell you about how and what God wants to give to you?

_____

_____

_____

_____

_____

Write out a prayer asking, seeking and knocking regarding what you are fasting for and who you are fasting for.

_____

_____

_____

_____

_____

_____

Day 19   Read Jeremiah 29:11-13 and Jeremiah 33:1-3

In Jeremiah 29 what does this tell you God has for you?

....

....

....

....

In Jeremiah 33 what does God want to tell you and show you?

....

....

....

....

....

....

How are you to seek Him?

....

....

....

....

Pray and ask God to tell you and show you the great and mighty things He has for you. Pray asking Him to show you the plans He has for you.

....

....

....

....

What have you learned about God during this Fast?

_____
_____
_____
_____
_____
_____

What have you learned about yourself during this Fast?

_____
_____
_____
_____
_____
_____

Write out a prayer asking God to move in the area of what you are fasting for.

_____
_____
_____
_____
_____
_____
_____
_____
_____
_____
_____

Day 20 Read Philippians 4:4-13

In verses 4-7 what are we told to do?

_____
_____
_____
_____
_____

What will be the result?

_____
_____
_____
_____
_____

In verses 8-9 what are we told to do?

_____
_____
_____
_____

What will be the result?

_____
_____
_____
_____

In verses 10-13 what does Paul tell you he has learned?

_____
_____
_____
_____

Write out a prayer rejoicing in Him and making your requests known to Him. Ask Him to give you contentment and His perfect peace.

_____

_____

_____

_____

_____

_____

Day 21 Read Ephesians 3:14-21

This is a prayer Paul prayed for all Christians. This is a prayer he prayed for you.

_____

_____

_____

_____

_____

Write down what Paul asked God to do for you.

_____

_____

_____

_____

How much of this is happening in your life?

_____

_____

_____

_____

Pray this prayer for yourself then go back and pray it for others in your life including the person you are fasting for.

_____

_____

_____

_____

Ask God during the fast to fulfill the requests of this prayer in your life in a way that is beyond description and beyond imagination.

_____

_____

_____

_____

Day 22 Read 2 Peter 1

What are we told God has given us in verse 3-4 and how is it given to us?

_____

_____

_____

_____

Look at verses 5-7 and write down what qualities Peter says we are to make sure we have. Pay attention to how these build on each other?

_____

_____

_____

_____

Write down what verses 8-11 tell us the results will be from having these qualities.

_____

_____

_____

_____

Look over the list of these qualities and ask God to reveal to you if any of these are not true in your life. Ask Him to tell you and show you how to make these a reality in your life.

_____

_____

_____

_____

Pray for God to say yes to the "something" you are fasting for.

_____

_____

_____

_____

Pray for the person you are fasting for.

_____

_____

_____

_____

_____

_____

_____

_____

Day 23 Read Jeremiah 9

Focus on verses 23-24.

_____

_____

_____

_____

_____

What are we told to not base our life on?

_____

_____

_____

_____

What are we told to base our life on?

_____

_____

_____

_____

What do we learn about God?

_____

_____

_____

_____

What does this passage tell you He delights in?

_____

_____

_____

_____

Ask God to reveal to you if you are basing your life on any of those things instead of on Him.

_____

_____

_____

_____

Write out a prayer asking God to help you know Him better and understand Him in a deeper way. As you do, write out anything that God brings to your mind.

_____

_____

_____

_____

Day 24 Read Romans 8:1-25

What do verses 6-8 tell you are the results of setting your mind on the flesh?

What does verse 6 say is the result of setting your mind on the Spirit?

Write down what verses 14-17 describe regarding the results of being led by the Spirit.

What does it mean to be led by the Spirit?

Pray and ask God if there is an area where your mind is set on the flesh. Write down anything God brings to mind.

Pray and ask God to fill you with the Holy Spirit and to cause you to be led by the Spirit.

....

....

....

....

....

Pray for the "something" you are fasting for and for the person you are fasting for.

....

....

....

....

....

Day 25 — Read Romans 8:26-39

What do verses 26-27 tell you the Spirit does for you?

What do verses 28-30 tell you God the Father does for you?

Who is the promise in verse 28 for?

Write down the promises you are to claim in verses 31-39.

According to verses 26-27, ask the Holy Spirit to intercede for you. Ask God for the things you do not know to ask for.

Ask God to turn to good anything that is not good in your life right now. Write down what you think that would be like.

_____

_____

_____

_____

_____

Take time to praise God that He turns all things to good and will make you more than a conqueror.

_____

_____

_____

_____

_____

Day 26 Read Matthew 5

The Beatitudes found in verses 1-12 are attitudes you are supposed to have.

_____

_____

_____

_____

Write down each of these attitudes and ask God to reveal to you how they apply to your life.

_____

_____

_____

_____

_____

What do verses 13-16 tell you that Jesus wants you to be?

_____

_____

_____

_____

Ask God to show you where you can be His salt and light. Ask Him to make you shine out for Him to the person you are fasting for.

_____

_____

_____

_____

_____

Day 27 Read Matthew 6

What do verses 5-15 tell you about prayer?

What do verses 16-18 tell you about fasting in light of what Jesus tells you in verse 1?

What do verses 19-24 tell you about money?

What do verses 25-34 tell you about worry?

In light of what you have read here, ask God to bring to mind any thoughts, habits or actions that need to change.

Write out a prayer for the person you are fasting for.

_____

_____

_____

_____

_____

Write out a prayer for what you are fasting for.

_____

_____

_____

_____

Day 28 Read Matthew 7

What do verses 1-5 tell you about how we are to look at others?

_____

_____

_____

_____

What does verse 12 tell you about how we are to treat others?

_____

_____

_____

What do verses 24-27 tell you about how we are to apply Jesus' words to our lives?

_____

_____

_____

_____

Ask God to reveal to you is you have a judgmental attitude toward anyone or even another group of people.

_____

_____

_____

_____

Ask God to bring to mind how you can treat someone in your life the way you would want them to treat you. Write down who God brings to your mind and what you could do for them.

_____

_____

_____

_____

Write out a prayer of commitment that you will truly be someone who acts on the words of Jesus and has a solid Spiritual foundation.

_____

_____

_____

_____

Pray for the person you are fasting for.

_____

_____

_____

_____

Day 29 *Read Luke 17*

Focus in on verses 5-10.

_____

_____

_____

_____

_____

What are the Apostles asking for in verse 5?

_____

_____

_____

_____

What does Jesus say increasing faith will be like in verse 6?

_____

_____

_____

_____

What does Jesus tell us leads to increasing faith in verses 7-10?

_____

_____

_____

_____

How does this tie in with what you read yesterday in Matthew 7:24-27.

_____

_____

_____

_____

_____

Ask God to increase your faith.

_____

_____

_____

_____

Commit to God that you will do ALL that He says.

_____

_____

_____

_____

Ask God if there is any area of your life that you are not being completely faithful in.

_____

_____

_____

_____

Pray for what you are fasting for and who you are fasting for.

_____

_____

_____

_____

Day 30   Read Matthew 10:24-25 and John 8:31-32

Write down Jesus' definition of what a disciple is from Matthew 10:24-25.

_____

_____

_____

_____

_____

Write down what is necessary for discipleship according to John 8:31-32.

_____

_____

_____

What do both passages tell you the result of discipleship is?

_____

_____

_____

How committed are you to having Jesus as Lord of your life?

_____

_____

_____

How passionate are you to become more and more like Jesus?

_____

_____

_____

_____

Write out a prayer asking God to help you submit every area of your life to Jesus' Lordship. Be sensitive to any prompting from the Holy Spirit about an area of your life you need to submit to Him.

_____

_____

_____

_____

_____

Write out a prayer asking God to mold you more and more into the image of Christ. What are some areas of your life where you need to see the image of Jesus being completely apparent?

_____

_____

_____

_____

_____

This week memorize Matthew 10:24-25.

_____

_____

_____

_____

_____

Day 31 Read John 13

What do we learn in verse 15?

How does that fit with what you read yesterday?

What are we told to do in verse 17 and what does that result in?

What is the new commandment we are to live by in verse 34?

What is the result of our living this out according to verse 35?

What are some ways that you can put on your "towel" to serve others and put their needs ahead of yours this week?

....

....

....

....

....

According to verses 34-35 a disciple loves like Jesus does. Pray for the people God has in your life and ask Him to bring to mind ways you can show the love of Jesus to them this week.

....

....

....

....

....

Pray for the person you are fasting for and ask God to give you an idea of a way you can reach out to them and show the love of Christ to them.

....

....

....

....

....

Day 32   Read John 15:1-11

In verses 1-11 what does Jesus call for us to do?

_____

_____

_____

_____

_____

What will be the results if we do what He asks?

_____

_____

_____

_____

What does verse 8 say about what another proof of discipleship is?

_____

_____

_____

_____

In verse 10 how does Jesus tell us we abide in His love?

_____

_____

_____

_____

Over the last 32 days are you being faithful to keep the commands of God? What is different in you now than when you started this fast?

_____

_____

_____

_____

_____

What changes are you making in your life? How have you changed?

_____

_____

_____

_____

_____

Pray and ask God to increase your faith and faithfulness to Him.

_____

_____

_____

_____

Pray and commit to abiding in His love and for His joy to be made complete in you.

_____

_____

_____

_____

Pray for what you are fasting for.

_____

_____

_____

_____

Day 33   Read John 15:12-27

In verses 12-17, what does Jesus tell us about our relationship with Him and each other?

According to verse 16 why did Jesus choose and appoint us?

In verses 18-25 what does Jesus tell us about our relationship with the world?

In verses 26-27 what does Jesus tell us about our relationship with the Holy Spirit? What does He do for us and what does He empower us to do?

Ask God to show you where and how you should bear fruit. Write out a prayer committing to God that you will be one who is faithful in seeking to be fruitful for Him.

_____

_____

_____

_____

Ask the Holy Spirit to bring to mind who you should be testifying to (sharing your Faith with). Pray for the people He brings to mind and write out a prayer asking for the Lord to give you opportunities to share with them this week.

_____

_____

_____

_____

Pray for who you are fasting for and ask God to give you an opportunity to share with them this week. Pray for ways that you can reach out to them.

_____

_____

_____

_____

Day 34   Read Philippians 2

In verses 1-4 write down how we are to relate to each other.

In verses 5-11 write down how Jesus is an example of relating in this way.

In verses 12-13 write down how we are to approach God and how He works in our lives. Why does He work this way with us?

In verses 14-16 write down how we are to live in this world.

Look back at Day 15 where we studied James 1. How does what you learned then go with what you are studying in verses 14-16?

According to what Paul tells us in Philippians 2, ask God to bring to mind some people whose needs you can put above your own. Ask Him how you can do so this week.

_____

_____

_____

_____

Ask God to help you be someone who never grumbles or complains. Write out a prayer asking for Him to make you a person of praise and not complaining.

_____

_____

_____

_____

Pray for what you are fasting for and praise God for the day He says yes!

_____

_____

_____

_____

Day 35 Read Isaiah 50

This is a prophecy of Jesus that He fulfilled completely. Read the chapter with Him in mind. Ask God to help you see how He lived and how he responded to the attacks and abuse that was inflicted on Him.

_____

_____

_____

_____

Write down what you learn about Jesus.

_____

_____

_____

_____

Write down what verses 4-5 tell you about being a disciple.

_____

_____

_____

_____

Pray and ask God to awaken you every morning with the sensitivity to hear His voice. Pray and commit to God that you will listen to what He says.

_____

_____

_____

_____

Pray for God to bring some people to mind who need to be given words of encouragement. Write down anyone God puts on your heart.

_____

_____

_____

_____

Ask Him to show you this week people you need to encourage and whose needs you need to put above your own.

_____

_____

_____

_____

Ask God to give you ideas for creative ways you can encourage them.

_____

_____

_____

_____

When you are able to encourage them, come back to this page and write down what you did and what happened when you did it.

_____

_____

_____

_____

Day 36   Read Isaiah 53

This is a prophecy about Jesus that He fulfilled completely. Read the chapter with Him in mind, asking God to help you really see who He was and what he went through for you.

_____

_____

_____

_____

What does verse 3 tell you about the feelings Jesus had while facing the cross?

_____

_____

_____

_____

In verses 4-6 what are we told that Jesus did for us and how did it affect Him?

_____

_____

_____

_____

According to verse 7, how did Jesus handle this?

_____

_____

_____

_____

What do verses 11-12 tell you would be the result of Jesus' suffering and dying for us?

_____

_____

_____

_____

_____

Write out a prayer praising Jesus and telling Him how much you love Him for bearing all of this for you.

_____

_____

_____

_____

_____

Pray for the person you are fasting for and ask that they would understand the sacrifice Jesus made for them.

_____

_____

_____

_____

_____

Day 37 Read Psalm 22

This is a prophecy of Jesus that was written before the Cross was even invented as a form of torture and capital punishment.

Write down how Jesus felt as He endured the Cross.

Write down what Jesus asked of the Father?

What do verses 22-23 call for us to do?

Write out a prayer of love and praise to Jesus for what He has done for you.

Look back at verses 11 and 19. Pray for God to be very near to You now and this week.

_____

_____

_____

_____

Look at verses 27-28. Write out a prayer asking God to make us all effective in bringing the name of Christ and His love to the nations of the earth. Ask God to prompt you to pray for a nation in particular.

_____

_____

_____

_____

Pray for what you are fasting for and for who you are fasting for.

_____

_____

_____

_____

_____

Day 38   Read John 17

This is the prayer Jesus prayed as He knew He would soon be going to the Cross.

_____

_____

_____

_____

Looking at verse 3, what is the definition of eternal life?

_____

_____

_____

_____

Read through verses 4-24 and list what Jesus prayed for.

_____

_____

_____

_____

Note verses 20-21 Jesus is including us in this prayer.

_____

_____

_____

_____

What do verses 24-25 tell us about why Jesus has made known the Father's name to us?

_____

_____

_____

_____

_____

How can you and I be answers to Jesus' prayer?

_____

_____

_____

_____

_____

Look back over the list of what Jesus prayed for and pray for what He desires to come to pass.

_____

_____

_____

_____

_____

Write down what the Spirit brings to mind as you pray for each of our Lord's heart's desires.

_____

_____

_____

_____

_____

Day 39   Read Luke 22

What does verse 15 tell you about how Jesus wants to have meaningful moments with us?

....

....

....

....

What is the vital lesson we need to learn and apply in verses 24-27?

....

....

....

....

Focus on verses 39-46. What are two key lessons we should learn and apply to our lives? What is the key to not entering into temptation?

....

....

....

....

Make a commitment to God that you will be prepared to have a special time with Him during communion this week when we are in Church together.

....

....

....

....

Ask God to show you how you can serve Him by serving someone else this week.

....

....

....

....

Take time to really pray the words... "Father, not my will but Your Will be done." As you pray this, be sensitive to what the Holy Spirit brings to mind. Are the areas of your life that you need to commit to reflecting the words, "not my will but Your Will be done"?

_____

_____

_____

_____

Write out a prayer of commitment. Commit to be someone who desires to be completely committed to God's Will for your life.

_____

_____

_____

_____

Pray for what you are fasting for and who you are fasting for.

_____

_____

_____

_____

Day 40   Read Luke 23-24

What stood out to you as you read chapter 23?

_____

_____

_____

_____

Focus in on Luke 24:13-35.

_____

_____

_____

_____

According to verse 21 what were they hoping Jesus would do for them?

_____

_____

_____

_____

What does Jesus point them to in verses 25-27?

_____

_____

_____

_____

What does verse 32 tell you about how they felt being in the presence of Jesus?

_____

_____

_____

_____

Ask Jesus to draw you near and disclose His presence to you now and the rest of this week.

_____

_____

_____

_____

Ask God to make you sensitive to His leading in your life.

_____

_____

_____

_____

Commit to the Lord that you will do His Will above all else.

_____

_____

_____

Pray for what you are fasting for and who you are fasting for.

_____

_____

_____

_____

Praise God that He will work His perfect Will regarding what you are fasting for and who you are fasting for.

_____

_____

_____

_____

_____

Day 41   Read Psalm 23

What have you learned in this time of fasting and praying.

_____

_____

_____

_____

_____

What has occurred in your relationship with God?

_____

_____

_____

_____

_____

How are you going to celebrate the end of the fast?

_____

_____

_____

_____

Did God say "yes" to what you fasted for?

_____

_____

_____

Did God do something in the life of the person you fasted for?

_____

_____

_____

_____

If you have not received an answer from the Lord yet, what did you learn on Days 17-18 that you are supposed to do? How does day 39 apply to this?

_____

_____

_____

Ask God to bring things to mind that He wants you to know. Sit and listen for what He is saying. Then write it down.

_____

_____

_____

_____

Write out a prayer to God committing to be completely His from this moment on.

_____

_____

_____

_____

_____

• • ● • •

I am so thankful that you have taken
this 40-day journey with the Lord.
I pray that He has granted you what you fasted for
and moved in the life of the person you fasted for.

Most of all I pray that you have taken a Next Step
in your walk with the Father.
I know when we do this that life is never the same.
God does love you and I have a passion for you
to grow closer and closer to Him.

• • ● • •